definitions

def·i·ni·tions | \ ˌdefəˈnish(ə)nz \
— *noun* —

definitions

def·i·ni·tions | \ ˌdefəˈnish(ə)nz \
— *noun* —

by Judith Kerman

Fomite
Burlington, VT

Copyright © 2021 by Judith Kerman

Published by   Fomite
                Burlington, VT
                www.fomitepress.com

ISBN 978-1-953236-17-3
Library of Congress Control Number 2020951087

ACKNOWLEDGEMENTS

Some of these poems appeared in:

Jewish Currents, Spring 2016

Aleph, broken: Poems from My Diaspora (Broadstone Books, 2016)

Like Light: 25 Years of Poetry & Prose by Bright Hill Poets & Writers (Bright Hill Press, 2017)

Facts, Fakes, & Fictions: Poems by Finalists in the 2018 Dora and Alexander Raynes Poetry Competition (Blue Thread Books, 2018)

Cover art by Katie McCann, *www.beetleblossom.com.* Author photo by Tim M. Inman. Book designed and typeset by Judith Kerman in Book Antiqua.

contents

con·tents | \ kənˈtentz \
— *noun* —

air
blues
conundrum
date
definition
elephant
fix
grief
handicap
ice
Judith
knot
lines
magic
metaphor
nonce
old
politics
queue
resistance
saw
shot
trade
unspeakable
vector
wry
xenophobia
yellow
zebra

zed
zenith
"Y"
xylophone
white
voice
utter
tart
still
snail
ream
queer
persistence
orbit
neophyte
mezzo
legs
Kerman
junk
Israel
home
geological
frost
eclipse
diaspora
cracker
cast
bat
apocalypse

I love English. There are so many things you can do with it.

– *Robert E. McDonough*

air

\ 'er \
— *noun; verb*

1. Walk out and breathe deeply:
   fresh scent of pine, leaf mold,
   rain coming. In August,
   first drops on road dust.

2. A lovely song, fresh and light,
   sometimes with variations.
   An aria. I fill my lungs, trying to
   feel my back ribs stretch
   for a full breath,
   an extended phrase.

3. Put it out for broadcast.
   We need more of it,
   flushing the dark rooms
   where politicians
   plot.

4. In winter,
   it bites.

blues

\ 'blüz \
— *adjective; noun* —

1. Shards of sky fallen from some nest.

2. Early Picasso.

3. Gainsborough's beautiful boy, satin and lace.

4. Indigo, a dyestuff grown by
   slaves sweating in the sun.

5. I remember new denims, too stiff
   to wear before washing.
   Now blue jeans are a luxury item,
   the more tattered, the better.

6. Truck-driver language.

7. An old man, blue-black, his voice a carpenter's rasp.
   His callused fingers talk to steel strings.
   He knows all about grief,
   betrayal. *Come back, sweet mama, come back.*

8. Mondays

conundrum

co·nun·drum | \ kə-'nən-drəm \
— *noun* —

1. How can it be
   that the self evaporates,
   rising like a wisp of steam off the body,
   diffused into air?
   One moment, a pudgy two-year-old,
   I respond, laughing, to my young mother,
   lovely in her high cheekbones and auburn hair.
   The next, there is no one there.

2. Someone is required to identify
   the body before burial,
   the *golem* without the sacred Name.
   In the open coffin, red lipstick my mother
   might have worn, white hair sprayed stiff
   as she would never do,
   only the bones of her face
   perhaps familiar.

3. I recall tying saddle-shoes,
   their white chalked with polish but still smudged,
   the back seat of the old black Studebaker,
   falling down stairs,
   dreaming of falling down stairs.
   Too late now
   to ask what they remembered:
   Daddy working in the family store after school,
   Mom and her aunt, new immigrants,
   smiling at the camera,
   squinting into the autumn sun.

date

\ 'dāt \
— *noun; verb* —

1. Small palm fruit, sometimes used
   to sweeten health foods.
   Doesn't taste like sugar to me.

2. Assignation or excursion,
   often assumed to be a meeting
   of potential lovers.

3. A solid, good looking person.
   Warm shoulder muscle under smooth shirt,
   warm dry hand.

4. Calendar page
   with the number circled in red.

5. The desired outcome
   of computer matching services.
   One guy loved *Moby Dick*, but didn't much care
   about my other interests. Another was
   a great Chinese cook,
   but lived with his mother.

definition

def·i·ni·tion | \ˌde-fə-ˈni-shən \
— *noun* —

1. Clarity of outline,
   the light at dawn
   limning each edge
   of building or tree.

2. Clarity of meaning.

3. Resolution of vision,
   the details through binoculars
   or microscope,
   or after squeezing in eye drops.

4. Dictionary entry, including etymology,
   pronunciation, usages.

5. My wish for certainty
   amid ambiguity.

elephant

el·e·phant | \ ˈe-lə-fənt \
— *noun* —

1. What no one in the room wants to talk about.

2. A large grey stone, heavy in the hand.

3. Handicap. Ugliness. Bigotry. Death.

4. Being blind, feeling your way around obstacles by touch, by smell.

5. Not a donkey.

6. The circus handlers urge their beasts to turn using big hooked sticks.
   It helps to have a thick skin,
   rough as tree bark.

7. They live in matriarchy,
   hold wakes for their dead.

fix

\ 'fiks \
— *noun; verb* —

1. The cat yowls all night,
   rolls, stretches, fore and aft.
   Time to take her to the vet.

2. We used to spend all night
   in the red light of the darkroom,
   watching images float up
   in the chemical bath.
   Digital makes it so convenient,
   but I miss the smell, the surprises.

3. Surgical consult, second surgical consult,
   physical therapy, acupuncture.
   Turmeric. Oxycodone. Medical marijuana.

4. A room full of
   big men with cigars; a quiet
   conversation over martinis
   or on the golf course.

grief

\ˈgrēf\
— *noun* —

1. Heavenly effort. When the sun rises,
   you will know what to do next.
   For now, try to sleep.

2. Sweet prickling at the ends of branches,
   nose turned
   into the warming air.

3. Searching. A long wait by a phone
   that does not ring.

handicap

hand·i·cap | \ 'han-di-ˌkap \
— *noun; verb* —

1. From Hand-in-cap, an English betting game
   too complicated
   to explain here.

2. Later, a competitive burden, such as
   weight added to a champion race horse
   to give the less-talented a fighting chance.

3. The number of strokes over par for the course
   considered appropriate for a duffer.
   At the tee, I consider mine.
   Very high and not likely to get
   any lower. I address the ball
   and swing. I whiff,
   hook, or slice.

4. In folk etymology, a crippled soldier
   on a street corner
   begging alms with his "cap in hand."

5. I'm now rewarded with a special tag
   for reserved parking spots.
   The new logo looks like everyone
   is a Paralympics athlete.

6. Some people don't like the term.
   Or "disabled" either.
   I just call myself
   "gimp."

ice

\ 'īs \
— *noun* —

1. In a glass
   it slowly turns to water.

2. Watch your step
   when you go out.
   Scatter rock salt,
   though it's bad for the grass.

3. What used to be
   la migra
   is now ICE —
   even colder at the heart.

4. As a kid, I went door to door
   repairing jewelry,
   collected rhinestones
   pried from costume settings.
   My parents promised diamonds
   when I was grown, but
   that never happened.
   I bought my own.

Judith

Ju·dith \ ˈjü-dəth \
— *proper noun* —

1. It was a popular name for babies in the 40's,
   perhaps because of *The Wizard of Oz*.
   Greatly declined since 1960.

2. Judy is diminutive of Judith,
   Hebrew, "she will be praised,"
   feminine of Judah.
   I was named for my uncle Jonathan,
   who died at the Bulge,
   but his Hebrew name was Yakov.

3. Did Cary Grant ever say,
   "Judy, Judy, Judy"?

4. A book of the Apocrypha.
   In a Jan Massijs painting, she holds aloft
   the severed head of Holofernes,
   dripping blood.

knot

\ 'nät \
— *noun* —

1. Up along the trunk,
   the tree has lost a branch,
   years ago, maybe, the scar
   grown in around heartwood.

2. Dark spot in the oak floor:
   beauty mark.

3. Traffic intersection,
   the kind called a "can of worms"
   or Malfunction Junction.

4. Marriage.

5. Conundrum. Alexander
   untied it with his sword.

6. Knitting, I pull yarn
   from the center of the ball.
   It comes out in a snarl
   to be picked apart
   with my fingernails.

7. My rough hair
   catches the comb.

lines

\ ˈlīnz \
− *noun* −

1. Bed sheets in the wind
   on a sunny day.

2. Poets worry about where to break
   them.

3. Prompters give you yours
   when you forget.

4. Loretta Young's face was a porcelain mask.
   We admired her on TV.
   My mother fussed at me even then
   about the lines in my forehead.

5. The old lady next door
   had fuzzy cheeks
   and creases like the ones I have now
   crossing her lips.
   Her lipstick crept up into the lines.
   Did she get them from whistling?

6. The only way to avoid lines
   is never to use your face
   for anything.

magic

mag·ic | \ 'ma-jik \
– *noun* –

1. When I was a kid
   I brewed together
   calamine lotion, Old Spice,
   Merthiolate. Evil smelling,
   orange and opaque.
   Dumped the evidence
   out my bedroom window.
   I killed a honeysuckle bush
   no one wanted.

2. The word is the wish,
   the soft nose of a horse
   nuzzling sugar from my palm.

3. The wish is the word.
   It flies with sapphire wings
   above the rooftops of houses
   where no one I know
   ever slept.

4. What can I do
   to make the world the way I want it,
   so that light rises into my window
   with silver in its pockets?

metaphor

met·a·phor | \ ˈme-tə-ˌfòr also -fər \
— *noun, from the Greek μεταφορά* —

1. Carriage, freightage,
   traction, traffic.
   A sign on the side of
   a moving van in Athens.
   Beds, bureaus, boxes of books.

2. The young tomcat
   tracks birds in the branches.
   His haunches
   prepare for launch.

3. I fold and float
   paper boats.

nonce

\ 'nän(t)s \
— *adjective; noun* —

1. For only one occasion.
   (Middle English.)

2. Word invented for a special use,
   although some nonce words
   later become common.
   For instance, "chortle."

3. Unique numeric token
   in cryptography.

4. Not once, according to some sources.
   Found in criminal pleadings of pedophiles.
   Hence, an insult.

5. A poem in a form
   never used before
   that may never be used again.

old

\ ˈōld \
– *adjective* –

1. Creased, wrinkled and stained.
   A book of no particular interest
   except for its leather binding,
   marbled endpapers.

2. Mellowed. Cheese or wine,
   dark colored and fragrant.

3. Creaky in the joints.
   When you go up the stairs,
   the wood groans.
   You also hear your knees.

4. Superannuated. Obsolete.

5. Nostalgic.

6. Wise but foolish. Foolish but wise.
   Once they thought old people were wise,
   then they thought we were senile, then
   they thought senility was confusion
   or medication. Now we call it Alzheimer's
   if we forget a word.

7. Vintage. A lace negligee from the 1920's,
   a desk made of real wood whose scars
   are from use. Anything
   that has gone out of fashion
   and is coming back in.

8. Never say "elderly,"
   at least not around me.

politics

pol·i·tics | \ 'pä-lə-ˌtiks \
— *noun* —

1. Yowling cats on either side of a glass door.

2. Knives in a blacked-out room.

3. A chickenyard. Red and black hens peck, squawk and flutter. No hawk in sight.

4. *A man, a bulldozer and a tree* (folk saying).

5. Fifty years of a bad marriage.

queue

\ 'kyü \
— *noun; homonym* —

1. Sounds like a pool stick
   or prompter's reminder.
   Also, the first letter of Quisling.

2. A Chinese hairdo in an old Western.
   A pigtail, from the French,
   "a long tail."

3. Where you have to wait a long time in England
   for a bus.

4. Question: Do you like Quisling?
   Answer: I don't know. I've never quisled.

resistance

re·sis·tance | \ ri-ˈzi-stən(t)s \
— *noun* —

1. When your back is up, you look and feel bigger.
   Ask any cat.

2. Tantrum. One ma's pretty baby
   is another ma's spoiled brat.

3. A very heavy rubber band
   used for building muscle.

4. Ohm's Law: Voltage divided by amperage.

5. The importance of the scheme
   multiplied by the number
   opposing it.

6. I used to imagine joining the Maquis.

saw

\ 'sȯ \
— *noun; verb* —

1. Jagged blade for cutting wood or metal.

2. What the old folks always say.

3. Up. Down. Up. Down.

4. *Margery daw, Johnny shall have a new master.*

5. What I should not have seen.

6. Cut off short.

shot

\ 'shät \
— *adjective; noun* —

1. Worn through into holes: old shirt, old shoes. Too far gone for Goodwill.

2. A hole in one. Nice!

3. Amber heat in the glass, a scent of oak.

4. And a beer.

5. Walking in the dark. Trees obscure the stars. A sound in the distance.

6. A 5-pound bag of steel pellets.

7. Look straight at the camera and don't move.

8. This won't hurt a bit.

trade

\ 'trād \
— *noun; verb* —

1. Exchange. Commerce. Swap meet.

2. In publishing, a "real" book,
   not a chapbook
   or nonstandard binding.

3. A sign in a shop window,
   meaning wholesale only.

4. Has been done with wives,
   husbands, children.

5. *In Amsterdam, there lived a maid —*
   mark well what I do say!
   In Amsterdam, there lived a maid
   and she was mistress of her trade.
   I'll no more go a-rovin' with thee, fair maid.

unspeakable

un·speak·able | \ ˌən-ˈspē-kə-bəl \
— *adjective* —

1. Once, perhaps, unsayable or unpronounceable.
   But word meanings
   drift.

2. The name of God in Hebrew.

3. In many cultures, private, unshared
   personal names.

4. Your grandfather's name
   when you're trying to pass.

5. Racial slurs, especially spoken by people in power,
   that used to be everyday expressions.

6. More recently, despicable, horrifying, as in
   the forcible separation of children
   from their parents.

vector

vec·tor | \ 'vek-tər \
— *noun* —

1. Direction, like the flight path
   of an arrow or poison dart.
   A mathematical abstraction.

2. Computers were invented
   to chart the trajectory of artillery.
   Only later were they used
   to track money.
   In computer graphics, vectors
   calculate a shape. Raster graphics
   have a space in memory
   for every pixel, like the retinas
   of our eyes.

3. The threat is invisible.
   Not mice and rats, but their fleas.
   Lice. Tick nymphs
   the size of poppy seeds.
   Doorknobs and elevator buttons.

4. Half the carriers have no symptoms,
   like Typhoid Mary,
   defiantly cooking for strangers.
   They go out in the street
   unmasked, insouciant:
   crowds at the beach in their bikinis,
   young men elbow to elbow at the bars.

5. The threat is like carbon monoxide,
   when the air in the house
   feels fresh, transparent,
   but the furnace guy says,
   "You coulda woke up dead!"

wry

\ 'rī \
– *adjective* –

1. Twisted, sometimes used to describe
   a stiff neck.

2. Funny or witty, but with a kink;
   the mouth smiling crookedly, the joke
   self-deprecating.

3. Not a staple cereal grain
   or what J. D. Salinger meant.

4. Rueful, with that slightly bitter taste.
   Like a seasoning, perhaps horseradish.

xenophobia

xe·no·pho·bia | \ ˌze-nə-ˈfō-bē-ə , ˌzē- \
— *noun* —

1. Sitting next to a young Mexican man on a plane,
   watching "Independence Day," I thought:
   this movie is about you.

2. Fear of things with armored, jointed arms:
   insects, crabs and spiders, especially big ones.
   This is why the extra-terrestrial in "Alien"
   looks like a huge bug,
   but "ET" doesn't.

3. Tinges our attraction to polar bears
   with their strange black noses
   and human-like curiosity.
   But we more closely resemble
   pandas and koalas.

4. Fear of halving the distance from a frontier,
   then halving it again.

5. Fear of the distance between me and my body.

6. Going into a crowd is OK if they all look alike.

7. They'd better look like me.

yellow

yel·low | \ 'ye-(ˌ)lō , dialectal 'ye-lər or 'ya- \
— *adjective; noun* —

1. A color attractive to bees and other pollinators.

2. Cowardly, especially in cowboy movies.

3. Snow you don't eat.

4. Certain newspapers.

5. Crayola color used for a smiling sun.

6. Cake made with egg yolks.

7. Ballpark mustard.

8. A burst of Forsythia.

9. About to turn red.

10. Do not cross this line.

zebra

ze·bra | \ 'zē-brə , Canadian and British also 'ze- \
— *noun* —

1. Football referee.

2. They tell medical students,
   "when you hear hoofbeats,
   don't think zebras."

3. Every one of them
   has a unique stripe pattern
   like fingerprints and snowflakes.

zed

\ˈzed \
— *noun* —

1. How the Brits say it.

2. The first letter of zoo. Zinger. Zoomorphic.

3. Dagwood Bumstead's nap; also sawing logs.

4. The caboose on the letter train.

5. A difficult first letter in an acrostic or Scrabble.
   A reason not to write Abcedarian poems.
   But X is harder.

6. In iconography, a lightning bolt
   or the mark of Zorro.

zenith

ze·nith | \ 'zē-nəth , Canadian also and British usually 'ze-nəth, -nith \
— *noun* —

1. An old radio with a plastic case.

2. High noon at the equator.

3. Opposite of nadir.

4. The peak of a career.
   It's all downhill from here.

"Y"

\ 'wī \
– *noun* –

1. A safe place
   to live for a while.

2. You can have fun there
   or work out. They have a pool.

3. In Spanish, the Greek "i"
   or the word for "and",
   but the Greek letter is an upsilon.

4. A famous poetry venue in New York City.
   Someday maybe I'll read there.

5. Why not?

xylophone

xy·lo·phone | \ 'zī-lə-ˌfōn also 'zi- \
— *noun* —

1.   A child's toy
   with colored metal plates,
   a musical crayon box.
   I don't remember having one.

2.   Marimba, often
   made of wood, as in
   xylem and phloem.

3.   In *Danse Macabre,* bones.
   Skeletons dancing.

white

\ '(h)wīt \
— *adjective; noun* —

1. Frozen tundra
   in a blizzard. Also, snow-blindness.

2. Bed sheet. Naval uniform.
   Tube socks before they're worn.
   The froth of a ballerina
   dancing the Dying Swan.

3. The space between stripes.

4. The arsenic once used to powder wigs.

5. Privilege.

6. Funeral flowers. Wedding dresses.

7. Conforming to tradition,
   devoid of spontaneity.
   Watered-down, censored,
   corrupt, ruthless. Redacted.

8. White is the color of my true love's hair.

9. Tasteless. Absent.

10. A group of people with skin color ranging
    from spray-paint orange to ivory-pale.

11. Eggshell, or "off".

voice

\ 'vòis \
– *noun, verb* –

1. Year after year,
   honey in my throat.
   Wanting to be heard,
   not wanting to be heard.

2. The work of an actor
   whose face is never on-screen.

3. Adjusting the tone of a piano
   or organ pipe.

4. Hounds on a scent.

5. Like Isaiah, crying: "Prepare Ye the way
   of the Lord!"

6. What people call "poetic voice"
   is a mystery to me.

7. I keep meeting people
   who were told as children
   not to sing.

utter

ut·ter | \ 'ə-tər \
— adjective; verb; noun —

1. Absolute, extreme or arrant,
as in, for example, the speeches
of most politicians.

2. Declare. Articulate. Expostulate.

3. Part of the name of a state in Northern India.

4. In Brooklyn, someone else.

5. A bad pun for mammary glands, which may
or may not be kosher,
depending on which part of Talmud you read.
One friend said you have to
cook it in a special pot,
udderly dedicated.

tart

\ 'tärt \
— *noun; adjective* —

1. A woman of unsavory reputation
   in a low-cut dress.

2. In the bakery, below the chocolate oak-leaf cookies:
   buttery, almond-flavored disks
   bigger than my hand, with fluted edges
   and a hole in the middle
   filled with raspberry jam.

3. Sharp-flavored, spicy, saucy.

4. Acid-tongued.

still

\ 'stil \
— *verb; noun; adjective; adverb; conjunction* —

1. To calm.

2. Straitjacket.

3. Copper coil attached to a boiler in a tumbledown cabin in the woods.

4. Two apples, cluster of grapes, brass candlestick, skull.

5. Single frame in a Muybridge sequence showing a horse with all four feet above the ground.

6. When the wind dies.

7. Emotionless. Dead.

8. Continuing.

9. Yet. Again. Nevertheless.

10. Moon over lake. Zen master.

snail

\ 'snāl \
— noun —

1. Tender as flesh
   under a fingernail, she
   extends her horns.

2. She seems in no hurry,
   exploring the stalks of tall grasses,
   making her own silver path,
   hauling her whorled house,
   burden and refuge,
   wherever she goes.

3. Her eggs gleam
   like seafoam in the sun.

ream

\ 'rēm \
— *noun; verb* —

1. 500 blank sheets of paper.
   There are no used "reams."
   A used ream is a manuscript.

2. First used in the 14th Century.
   Derived from separate contrasting words
   for to bundle and
   to enlarge an opening.

3. Using a tool to clean out a pipe
   or other hollow object.

4. When your boss rips you out a new one.

queer

\ 'kwir \
– adjective; verb; noun –

1. Once a word for odd.
   Peculiar. Unusual.

2. In some dialects,
   milk that has soured.

3. An agreement that has
   gone bad, queering the deal.

4. *Once our good King Henry gave a spread*
   with all his pals and gals, a ghastly crew.
   The headsman carved the joint and cut the bread.
   Then in came Anne Boleyn to queer the do!

5. It did not always imply unsavory,
   although perhaps
   deviant.

6. The achievement of noun status
   is a point of pride.

7. LGBTQ+.

8. I choose Plus.

persistence

per·sis·tence| \ pər-'si-stən(t)s , -'zi- \
— *noun* —

1. *Hoya.* Species *carnosa,* "fleshy."
   The blossoms burst,
   fireworks, each floweret at the end
   of its radiating stalk
   a tiny five-pointed waxy star
   with a dark red circle at its center.

2. For years, it sat in my windowless office
   on a high shelf near a fluorescent light,
   never watered but persisting.
   I didn't think it could bloom,
   and it never did
   until I brought it home to a bright window,
   watered it sparingly.

3. Now, I know not to clip the tendrils
   that sprawl their leathery almond-shaped leaves
   across my desk.
   It will bloom again from the same node.
   Soon it may drip sweet nectar.

4. Late at night, I smell its heavy perfume,
   which it breathes out
   only in the dark.

orbit

or·bit | \ ˈȯr-bət \
— *noun; verb* —

1. Out in the Oort cloud,
   floating planetoids and ice balls,
   it's cold, and the Sun gleams
   barely brighter than Sirius.

2. Galileo was named a heretic
   for understanding orbits.

3. My Jewish life, like a comet,
   swooped in from far places
   close around the warmth:
   m'shpuchah and chicken soup,
   Hebrew and *niggun*.
   I brightened,
   wore fringed corners,
   learned the rituals and songs.
   But lately, I've been headed back out..

4. Where a comet once traveled,
   fragments follow the old path,
   enter the atmosphere
   as meteors, flashing
   across the night sky.

neophyte

neo·phyte | \ ˈnē-ə-ˌfīt \
— *noun* —

1. Algae bloom.

2. A maple's helicopter seed.

3. Young sprout,
   wet behind the ears.

4. Jealous lover.

5. Apprentice or intern.

6. Farm team.

7. Bud dreaming of flowers.

mezzo

mez·zo | \ 'met-(,)sō , 'med-(,)zō \
— *adjective; noun* —

1. The notes where
   my voice glides.

2. A balancing pole
   on the high wire
   teeters above the crowd.

3. The broken stem of a reed
   creases
   a puddle's skin.

4. Where a book's wings
   meet the spine.

5. Where a three-line poem
   breathes.

6. On the street,
   a yellow line.

legs

\ 'legz also 'lāgz \
— *noun* —

1. Nickname for a chorus girl.

2. On Broadway, lasting long enough to make money for the investors.

3. Famous gangster.

4. A table relies on them. Ball and claw. Gate leg. With or without casters.

5. Where the most complex joints and longest bones are.

6. What propels most athletes.

7. Visible means of support.

8. Part of a relay race. I'm out.

9. Endurance.

10. A wheelchair is a poor substitute.

Kerman

Ker·man | \ kər-ˈmän , ker- \
— *proper noun* —

1. A province in Persia
   known for a certain type
   of formal rug.

2. I was told my ancestor Epstein
   was adopted by a widow Kerman.
   As her only son, he'd be exempt
   from the Czar's army.
   I haven't yet found this in the family tree.

3. There are Kermans from England, Saxons perhaps,
   from Low German, *church warden*.
   (Yiddish is a different Low German.)
   I met some of them among the Quakers.
   Different lineages with similar lifestyles,
   like hummingbirds and bumblebees:
   convergent evolution.

4. Another Judith Kerman phoned me once
   to congratulate me on a scholarship.
   This was not a hoax.
   Her father was Bert and mine was Harry
   like the brothers in the Piels beer ad.

5. Not Kierman, Kernan, Kermit, Kevin,
   Kirman with an "i" anywhere, or
   Carmen.

junk

\ 'jəŋk \
— *noun; adjective; verb* —

1. A Chinese boat with sails like Venetian blinds.
   A carved dragon figurehead and dragons
   painted on the sides
   bring luck in bad storms.

2. Dealers huddle on street corners
   in bad parts of town,
   doing business with sad children.

3. Accumulates in back rooms, closets, sheds
   and kitchen drawers. Once, an old man
   driving a spavined horse and cart
   went door to door, collecting,
   calling to housewives looking out the windows.
   Now, on reality TV, two guys
   driving a spiffy white van
   visit hoarders to dig for treasure.

4. What hangs between a man's legs.

5. To: Occupant

6. Don't hang up.
   This is not a sales call.

Israel

Is·ra·el | \ 'iz-rē-əl , -(,)rā- also 'is- or 'iz-rəl \
— *noun* —

1. The national name of the Hebrew people; see also Jew, Israelite.

2. Dreaming. History.

3. Jacob after he dreamed.

4. An infected cut that pulls when I stretch, throbs at rest.

5. A settler state.

6. Where we will be safe if all else fails.

7. What I wrestle with.

8. Love and fear, meeting on a desert road and making peace.

9. The land belongs to No One. We walk on it and draw lines. *Mine!* we declare in that toddler voice.

10. Blood ties. And blood.

home

\ 'hōm \
— noun; verb —

1. In a ballpark, everyone's goal. Five-sided like a child's drawing of a house, but without the chimney.

2. Chicken soup with dill and eggs that had not yet been laid.

3. Sports photographers used to send out their film by carrier pigeon. Now they use drones and an uplink.

4. *The place where, when you have to go there, they have to take you in.*
   — Robert Frost

5. A cardboard box and a shopping cart.

6. Where the heat-seeking missile goes.

7. For an exile, no place.

geological

geo·log·i·cal | \ ˌjē-ə-ˈlä-ji-kəl \
— *adjective* —

1. Eroded. Crevassed. Weathered, sun-blasted,
   twisted like the surface of a lava flow.
   Marine iguanas, the same crusty black,
   stained white by the salt they excrete,
   tear ducts driven to extremes.

2. Look into a mirror:
   pocked, granulated, puckered, water-worn.
   Sediment in the corners.

3. Brittle, like volcanic tufa. Undercut and toppling.
   My feet hesitate, my sense of balance
   falters on uneven ground, rocky places.

4. Gneiss, schist, solidified under pressure.
   Coal seam, gold vein.
   Diamond pipe, a vanished mountain's throat
   standing above the veldt.

5. The river and the rain
   are always young. The bones
   already old.

frost

\ ˈfrȯst \
— noun —

1. The first cold night
   nips still-living leaves.

2. Driving through western Pennsylvania
   on what looks like dry pavement,
   I see a car spin out.

3. I raise the blinds in the morning.
   Where the glass meets the sash,
   frozen moisture begins to melt.

4. Feathered lines crawl over my cheeks,
   dry as an apple-face doll
   carved with a pen-knife
   and left to shrivel on a windowsill.

eclipse

\ i-'klips \
— *noun; verb* —

1. In theater, a bit player
   upstages the star.

2. The vortex draws the eye
   up and in.
   No one is weeping.
   The dog in the next car
   stares at the sky,
   does not bark.

3. The sky is not black
   but the luminous blue of dusk.
   Firefly Venus floats beside
   the circle of sun-moon,
   a Ceylon sapphire
   set in diamonds.

4. Blood moon.

diaspora

di·as·po·ra | \ dī-ˈa-sp(ə-)rə , dē- \
— *noun* —

1. A woman with a kerchief over her hair
   sits on a suitcase. Somewhere,
   going somewhere else.

2. Distance. The idea of homecoming. Were we taken, or did we go?

3. The smells of cooking hover in the stairwells.
   The roof leaks.

4. Suburbia.

5. In each generation, scattered like dandelion fluff, the tiny parachute that takes the seed to a place where it might root. The dandelion has a deep taproot. It does not want to move again.

6. Visiting the "old country," we carry phrasebooks and maps of the sacred places.

7. Mitzvah-mobiles: backpacks, valises, tents,
   the movable sanctuary, the Ark
   with its carrying poles.

8. In the book *Nomadic Furniture,* everything folds up or is disposable. Armchairs made of corrugated cardboard. Air mattresses.

9. Don't buy too many books.

cracker

crack·er | \ 'kra-kər \
— *noun* —

1.   A round disk with scalloped edges
   and pinholes in the top,
   slightly greasy, whose artificial butter taste
   remains with me
   all these years later.
   I ate them
   out of the box.

2.   An insulting name,
   for a white Southerner,
   one of many words
   forbidden in our family.

3.   As a young child, looking down
   from our apartment window
   to the park at dusk, I saw older kids
   setting off firecrackers on the benches.
   I remember small squares of fire,
   shaped like saltines.

cast

\ˈkast\
– adjective; noun; verb –

1. Iron railing or skillet.
   Woodstove.

2. Negative space where the wax
   runs out and the molten bronze
   flows in.

3. The accused adulteress
   is buried in sand
   up to her neck.
   A stone delivers
   a last kiss.

4. An elegant feathered fly
   snags the trout.

5. The stone
   skips three times across the water.

6. A broken wrist,
   held rigid as it heals,
   itches and sweats.

7. Two heroes, one *femme fatale*,
   three supporting actors,
   twelve spear-carriers.

8. Death mask.

bat

\ 'bat \
— verb; noun —

1. Heavy oak or ash,
   narrow waist, clubbed head.
   Not since high school have I felt
   that heft in my hand,
   the pull of it in my shoulders
   as I swing.

2. One night, the student renting my upstairs room
   ran down, shouting about a big black bird.
   The "Bat Man" installed one-way valves
   so bats could fly out
   but not come back.

3. *...y en tu menudo cuerpo*
   caben dos glorias que jamás unen
   en otro ser: alas y pecho."
   (...and in your small body
   two glories fit that never unite
   in another being: wings and breasts.
           — Dulce María Loynaz, tr. JBK

4. Bats in cages in a Chinese market
   may have been the source of Covid-19.

5. The cat's paw targets
   anything that moves.

6. She hunts in the high dark,
   nurses her young
   as she hangs on the wall.

apocalypse

apoc·a·lypse | \ ə-ˈpä-kə-ˌlips \
— *noun* —

1. The ruined temple of the goddess Calypso, once the center of her cult. Located at the highest point of the city Calypsos, of which she was patroness. Destroyed during a 50-year war with a neighboring city-state. The sun has blasted the bas-reliefs of her warrior kings.

2. A scrubby tree of semi-arid regions with grey-green foliage and a peculiar but pleasant pungency. Often used in dry flower arrangements. The main food of *Ursus teddyus*, a small plush-furred quadruped. They sit in pairs among the branches, endlessly grooming each other.

3. A type of speech impediment characterized by excessive sibilance. Thought to have been the sound made by certain ancient prophetesses when under the influence of their deity.

4. A set of books containing names omitted or expunged from the New York Telephone Directory, held by certain groups to be the true record of the population. On sacred occasions, the names are read out in the city squares.

author

au·thor | \ 'ȯ-thər \
— *noun* —

Judith Kerman is a poet, clown (Reb Kugel, the Rubbadubdubber Rebbe), singer and artist. She has published ten books or chapbooks of poetry, most recently *Aleph, broken: Poems from My Diaspora* (Broadstone Books, 2016), three books of translations of Spanish Caribbean women, and two scholarly anthologies. Kerman was a Fulbright Senior Scholar to the Dominican Republic in 2002, translating Dominican women writers and researching Dominican folkways. In addition to learning Dominican papier-maché mask making, she filmed, wrote and edited a 24-minute video, *Dominican Carnaval*, visible on YouTube. After a career in university teaching and administration, she moved to Woodstock, NY, where she runs Mayapple Press. She founded *Earth's Daughters* magazine in Buffalo, NY, which has been published regularly since 1971.

Fomite

More poetry from Fomite...

Anna Blackmer — *Hexagrams*
L. Brown — *Loopholes*
Sue D. Burton — *Little Steel*
David Cavanagh— *Cycling in Plato's Cave*
James Connolly — *Picking Up the Bodies*
Greg Delanty — *Loosestrife*
Mason Drukman — *Drawing on Life*
J. C. Ellefson — *Foreign Tales of Exemplum and Woe*
Tina Escaja/Mark Eisner — *Caida Libre/Free Fall*
Anna Faktorovich — *Improvisational Arguments*
Barry Goldensohn — *Snake in the Spine, Wolf in the Heart*
Barry Goldensohn — *The Hundred Yard Dash Man*
Barry Goldensohn — *The Listener Aspires to the Condition of Music*
R. L. Green — *When You Remember Deir Yassin*
Gail Holst-Warhaft — *Lucky Country*
Raymond Luczak — *A Babble of Objects*
Kate Magill — *Roadworthy Creature, Roadworthy Craft*
Tony Magistrale — *Entanglements*
Gary Mesick — *General Discharge*
Andreas Nolte — *Mascha: The Poems of Mascha Kaléko*
Sherry Olson — *Four-Way Stop*
Brett Ortler — *Lessons of the Dead*
David Polk — *Drinking the River*
Janice Miller Potter — *Meanwell*
Janice Miller Potter — *Thoreau's Umbrella*
Philip Ramp — *The Melancholy of a Life as the Joy of Living It Slowly Chills*
Joseph D. Reich — *A Case Study of Werewolves*
Joseph D. Reich — *Connecting the Dots to Shangrila*
Joseph D. Reich — *The Derivation of Cowboys and Indians*
Joseph D. Reich — *The Hole That Runs Through Utopia*
Joseph D. Reich — *The Housing Market*
Kenneth Rosen and Richard Wilson — *Gomorrah*
Fred Rosenblum — *Playing Chicken with an Iron Horse*
Fred Rosenblum — *Vietnumb |*
David Schein — *My Murder and Other Local News*
Lawrence Schimel — *Desert Memory: Poems of Jeannette L. Clariond*
Harold Schweizer — *Miriam's Book*
Scott T. Starbuck — *Carbonfish Blues*
Scott T. Starbuck — *Hawk on Wire*
Scott T. Starbuck — *Industrial Oz*
Seth Steinzor — *Among the Lost*
Seth Steinzor — *To Join the Lost*
Susan Thomas — *In the Sadness Museum*

Fomite

Susan Thomas — *The Empty Notebook Interrogates Itself*
Sharon Webster — *Everyone Lives Here*
Tony Whedon — *The Tres Riches Heures*
Tony Whedon — *The Falkland Quartet*
Claire Zoghb — *Dispatches from Everest*

Writing a review on social media sites for readers will help the progress of independent publishing. To submit a review, go to the book page on any of the sites and follow the links for reviews. Books from independent presses rely on reader-to-reader communications.

For more information or to order any of our books, visit:
http://www.fomitepress.com/our-books.html

www.ingramcontent.com/pod-product-compliance
Lightning Source LLC
Chambersburg PA
CBHW021451070526
44577CB00002B/359